The Employing Positively Series

Employing Care Staff in Your Home

Employing doesn't need to be a hassle.
An easy-to-use guide of the things to know and do

CECILY LALLOO

Copyright ©2021 Cecily Lalloo

ISBN: 978-1-4478-4948-3

All rights reserved. No part of this publication may be reproduced, distributed or transmitted in any form or by any means, including photocopying, recording, or other electronic or mechanical methods, without the prior written permission of the publisher, except in the case of brief quotations embodied in critical reviews and certain other non-commercial uses permitted by copyright law. For permission requests, write to the publisher, addressed:
'Attention: Permissions Coordinator' at the email address below.

welcome@hilfranpublishing.com

Any references to historical events, real people, or real places are used fictitiously. Names, characters and places are products of the author's imagination.

All trademarks, service marks, registered trademarks and registered service marks are the property of their respective owners and are used herein for identification purposes only.

Cover and images by: Rayhaan Jassat

Published by HilFran Publishing
First printing edition 2021

Author: Cecily Lalloo
Buckinghamshire
United Kingdom
HP21

www.hilfranpublishing.com

This book is dedicated to my Dad,
Francis Cilliers Grainger-Rousseau, a gentleman,
an educationalist, a role model. He wanted to write his memoirs
but never did.

May he rest peacefully and look upon my attempt at putting
words into a book as a dedication to him.
May this be the first of many.

Love you Dad

08.11.1906 – 16.10.1984

Acknowledgements

My gratitude is extended to so many people without whom this book would not have been published. They have encouraged me, provided advice and guidance and just been there.

Let me start with my mentor, Eloise, without whom I'd still be procrastinating and wondering 'how to'. Also Rayhaan for patiently working on graphics, from logo to cover design and all images. Robert for his attention to detail, his advice and continuing support. Bridgette, Carol, Deana, Nath, Manisha, Maybelle and Robert for persevering and reading through early manuscripts and providing much-needed feedback. Laura for editing, proofreading and providing her expertise. Nate for the web design and coaching on web stuff. All my family, Pri, Tricia, Manisha, Sebastian, Denise, Gail, Malcolm, Timothy and their spouses, my nieces and nephews. My late brother Gavin. To all my extended family and friends who I've not seen or contacted for a while because my head has been buried in this project. And last, but by no means least, to Dhiru, for allowing me to get on and 'do it', for playing devil's advocate, and just being there. Thank you so much.

You have all been supportive and encouraging when it was an uphill trudge. I am extremely grateful to you for the part you have played in this, my first publication.

Contents

Acknowledgements	4
Contents	5
Preface	8
Introduction	10
1: Recruit and Select	15
2: The Employment Relationship	25
3: The Onboarding Process	33
4: Maintaining the Employment Relationship	40
5: Time off Work	46
6: Dealing with Workplace Problems	55
7: Leaving	63
8: Keeping Records	75
9: Useful Information	80
10: About the Author	82

Preface

The care sector covers a very broad range and there are many, many people working in this sector. I have worked in a niche area of care since 2013, providing HR (human resources) advice and support to the clients of deputies who have been appointed by the Court of Protection. I have also worked and provided support to case managers, and to individual adults. I have gained so much knowledge and experience that I want to share some of it.

This book is written to help parents, families and individuals who hire and manage paid care staff to work in their private homes. In the normal course of events, we do not expect to employ care staff in our homes. Yet, in the real world, accidents and illness happen, and sometimes adults or children require care because they are unable to care for themselves. We know that this is a traumatic time for families.

I have provided HR support for families whose children (the client), through acquired brain injury, need care staff, sometimes on a 24-hour basis. I have also provided HR support for adults (the client) who have acquired a brain injury or spinal injury and who need care staff on a 24-hour basis, or who simply need a buddy now and again.

When carers work in a private home, they get to know the client well. It is not surprising that relationships form and the care staff almost become part of the family. However, when paying someone to work, the role of employer and employee must be clear. Boundaries and rules are helpful so as to meet expectations on both sides.

In my experience, the issues relating to employment in a care setting in a private home are the same as employment issues in any business.

My aim in this book is to share my knowledge and experience with parents, families and individuals who need care staff in their homes, so that the employment experience is positive and does not cost more than it should.

Deputies and case managers may find it a useful resource to share with their clients.

It must be noted that the law changes continuously and this book is not intended to replace professional advice.

This book is set out so you can easily read by topic and it can be picked up and put down as needed. If you would like to read about different or other topics, I would love to hear from you.

I hope you find it helpful and I very much look forward to your reviews. My contact details are included at the back of the book.

Introduction

Whether you are a parent, a family member or an adult in need of care, looking to hire specialist care to support you or a member of your family, this book is for you. This book will also be useful for case managers and deputies to share with their clients.

The book aims to provide information on HR matters that may mitigate the risk of financial loss, which could diminish the resources of the person in need of care. If you already have specialist care, this book is for you too.

Adults who require care and parents of children who require care are often time-stretched for various reasons, perhaps because they are also running a home, working, running a business, or caring for other children. As a result, minor employment issues are not addressed with staff in a timely manner. This can result in employment disputes that can take up much time, as well as cause emotional distress and financial loss.

Advice must be sought from HR experts when there is a potential employment dispute. Advice sought before a dispute is valuable. HR advice sought at the beginning of an employment relationship is even more valuable.

Throughout this book, we refer to the 'HR expert'. This expert can be an employment law solicitor, an HR consultant, an employment advice line, or one of the other organisations set out in Chapter 9: Useful Information.

When employing, it is recommended that legal expenses insurance is bought. When an employer ends an employment relationship there are certain procedures that must be followed to ensure a fair dismissal and to manage the risk of unfair dismissal claims being brought to an employment tribunal. The financial, emotional and physical costs associated with managing a case that is brought can be high. Legal expenses insurance can be helpful.

Different types of employment

There are different ways that staff work, dependent on the type of contract or agreement they have. Staff could work through an agency, or they could work directly for a family or individual, or on a casual 'as needed' basis.

In this book, we refer to people who work on a casual non-employed basis as 'workers'. Workers[1] are not guaranteed work. They may or may not be offered work and, when they are offered work, they do not need to accept.

Directly employed staff can be permanent employees who are offered a minimum number of contractual hours. Alternatively, they can be employed on a zero-hours basis where they are not guaranteed any contractual hours. This is known in the sector as a 'zero-hours contract'.

It is a good idea to discuss with an HR expert how you want a carer to work so that the appropriate contractual document can be drawn up.

---

[1] A 'worker' in employment terms has some employment rights, including written terms, national minimum wage, paid holiday, payslips, protection for whistleblowing, protection against unlawful discrimination and the right not to be treated unfairly if working part-time (acas.org).

A contract of employment [2] (or contract) will be referred to for directly employed staff in this book, while an agreement is referred to in the case of workers, as described above.

The employment scenarios in this book

In this book, there are two types of employment situations that can apply.

First, carers are required for an adult or a child. The adult or parents of the child will be the direct employer of care staff. This is a straightforward situation.

In the second scenario, a claim for personal injury may have resulted in a financial settlement for an adult or a child. The Court of Protection (CoP) then appoints a deputy to act on behalf of that person because they cannot manage their own affairs due to injury and/or they are a minor. In this case:

- The deputy can therefore be considered the employer, acting on behalf of the client
- The deputy may set up a trust and parents may be included as trustees
- The deputy may appoint a case manager to manage the client's wellbeing
- The case manager will work with others to ensure the wellbeing and care of the client, including those working with the family (physiotherapists, speech therapists, psychologists, social services, schools or colleges, and HR advice and support) who, together, may be seen as a multi-disciplinary team (MDT)

---

[2] A contract of employment or employment contract is also known as a written statement of particulars.

- The case manager will recruit carers and manage them as their line manager
- Where there are many carers, the case manager may appoint a team leader
- As the case manager is not at the client's home on a daily basis, a parent is often the first point of contact for carers
- Some parents have delegated authority from the deputy to carry out the team leader role

With such a complex organisational structure, it is essential that an HR expert is part of the team to provide advice and support on employment matters.

Employing need not be a hassle

Employing does not need to be a hassle if you know the basics, follow procedures and, wherever possible, follow best practice.

There is much to think about when you employ people. This book takes you through the employee lifecycle. It touches on different aspects of employing and points to useful information and people that can help. It is not intended to overwhelm you with detailed employment law regulation. Instead, it provides the information and answers you need to manage your staff proactively.

Each section sets out an introduction to the topic, various checklists, a case study and five top tips to quickly summarise the content of the chapter.

The employee lifecycle

In everything in life, there is a start, a middle and an end, and this is also true of the employee lifecycle. The start is when you recruit; the end comes in different ways; and a lot happens in the middle between the start and the end.

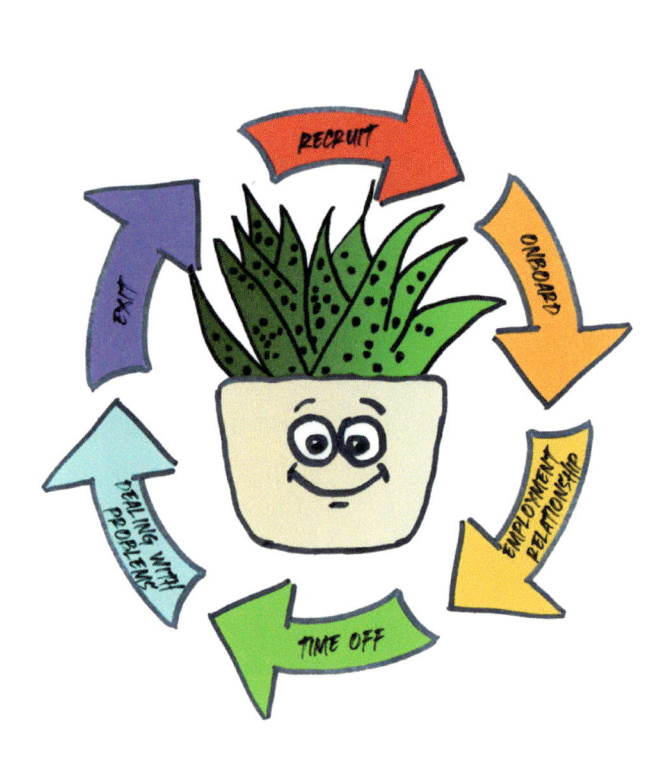

1: Recruit and Select

Finding the right people is the basis for success in any workplace. We have all heard the phrase 'people are our most valuable asset'. It is important therefore to decide who will carry out the recruiting. This could be a case manager, parents, the HR expert or a recruiter. It pays to spend time with the recruiter to discuss the type of person who is needed, what experience, skills and qualifications they require, and what work they will be doing.

When people are needed, it is usually immediate. This becomes an intense time for the employer looking for help and for the person seeking work. Take time on an annual basis to contemplate whether more or less staff are needed and plan if you can. Capture requirements in a job description and person specification. This will help you with advertising and when you interview.

The job description

We are naturally attracted to those who are similar to us - this is called the 'halo effect'. You may miss the ideal person if you have not set out your expectations in a job description. Different people will bring a different dynamic to the role. There are many examples of job descriptions and job specifications. Find the one that best suits you and take advice from an HR expert or a recruiter.

Permanent employee or worker

Do you need a carer on a permanent basis? Can you provide regular hours of work? If so, a permanent carer would be best. An employment relationship is developed when there is a mutual obligation for the employer to provide work and for the employee to carry out that work and receive payment for it.

If you have enough carers for regular work and you want someone to be available when one of your regular carers is away, for instance on holiday, a worker may be best so you can call on them as and when you need. You do not guarantee that you will offer them regular work, and they do not need to accept the work when you offer it. However, if you offer work on a regular basis and it is accepted by the worker regularly, you should know that you may form an employment relationship where the worker will have similar contractual rights to the permanent employee.

There are differences in the employment rights and obligations of an employee and a worker. However, in general terms, in this book, the word 'employment' is used to refer to both the conventional employer/employee relationship and the employer/worker relationship. If you are unsure about the employment status of the carer, discuss this with your HR expert.

Attitude versus skill

Remember that the person needs to fit in with you and your family. They may not tick all the boxes in terms of your job description, but the person with the right attitude can usually be trained. It's more difficult to change an attitude, so choose someone who has the behaviours and attitude you need and train for skills wherever you can.

Right to work

Ensure that all candidates' documents are checked for the right to work in the country. You should establish this as early as possible, preferably in the first interview, but definitely before they start work. Information can be found on the gov.uk website.

Advertise

When advertising, ensure that you do not discriminate using language that might exclude people with protected characteristics; these are set out in the Equality Act 2010. The Equality Act protects employees and workers from discrimination or unfair treatment on the basis of personal characteristics, which are *age, disability, gender reassignment, marriage and civil partnership, pregnancy and maternity, race, religion or belief, sex and sexual orientation.*

When inviting candidates to interview, ask whether reasonable adjustments should be considered. For example, someone who has a hearing impairment may need a hearing loop. Do not make judgements based on a disability or names on a CV or application form. Ask all candidates the same questions so that each has a chance to respond and you can compare like for like.

If your requirement is for female carers only, for example, you should state in the advertisement that it is an exception to the Equality Act. The reason for exceptions must be clear and reasonable. Seek professional advice if the job search excludes anyone with the above protected characteristics.

Many jobs in the care sector are offered on a part-time basis. Employees who work part-time must not be treated less favourably[3] than their full-time colleagues in relation to pay and benefits. For instance, if they work 20 hours a week and a colleague works 40 hours a week, their pay should be proportional to the person working 40 hours. This is referred to as 'on a pro rata basis'.

Does your advert compare favourably to other jobs advertised in your area? Have you provided enough relevant information to attract applicants?

---

[3] The Part-Time Workers (Prevention of Less Favourable Treatment) Regulations 2000 refers to the fact that a part-time worker must not be treated less favourably than a full-time worker.

Checklist for advertising

- Set a date to start and finish the advert
- Outline the job title
- Confirm the pay details
- Provide information on the location
- Describe the person for whom care is required
- Set out the shift pattern – days and times
- List benefits like sick pay and holidays
- Describe essential requirements, such as DBS check and driver's licence; and desirable requirements, such as Level 3 Health and Safety
- Describe responsibilities and tasks, e.g. personal care, administering medication, record-keeping
- Set out the person specifications; for instance, what characteristics and qualities are important, e.g. punctuality, honesty, positive outlook, enjoys outdoor activities, organised

Where to advertise

There are many suitable places to advertise. Consider where the ideal people might look for jobs. The majority of job-seekers use the internet as there is a proliferation of job sites, recruitment agencies and social media platforms that advertise.

If the job role is for a few hours or a few days, it may be preferable to post adverts in local shops, post leaflets through letterboxes, or talk to family, friends or members of staff. Below are some methods to use to recruit:

- Place a postcard advert in local shops or schools
- Use online job boards
- Promote jobs on social media such as Facebook, Twitter and LinkedIn
- Word of mouth is a powerful recruitment tool
- Advertise through agencies

Checklist for interviewing and selection

If you intend to interview, be prepared. It is a good idea for at least two people to interview so that your observations can later be discussed. Below is a list of things to keep in mind when interviewing and selecting.

- Send an application form to candidates
- Prepare for the interview: read the job description and use it as a prompt
- Write/type out questions
- Decide who will interview
- Set aside dates for interviews – will they be by phone, video call or face-to-face
- To avoid the risk of discrimination, ask open questions based on job requirements
- Do not ask questions or base your decisions on the protected characteristics mentioned in Five Top Tips at the end of this Chapter
- What experience is essential, for instance is a night-worker required, or experience of working with children with complex needs
- Draft the invitation to interview
- Collect personal data such as email address
- Send unsuccessful candidates a response
- Invite shortlisted, successful candidates promptly to further interviews or assessments
    - Assessments can take the form of observing the candidate's interaction with the client and completing simple tasks to check competence
    - Assessments are part of the recruitment and selection process and should not be used for training

Here is a selection of questions that may be asked:

- We have to ask everyone this question – do you have the right to work in the UK? We need to see your documents or gain your consent to check your status online.
- Do you have an appropriate DBS for an adult or child workforce?
- What attracted you to this job?
- The job requires moving and handling, a lot of floor work. Can you describe the experience you have had with this type of work?
- You state that you have a certificate in Level 2 – what did you enjoy on this course? May I see your certificate?
- The working pattern is from [day] to [day]. Does this suit you?
- What is your notice period to leave your current job?
- Do you have any holiday booked in the next few weeks so I can plan further interviews and assessments?

Also, ask searching questions to provide a picture of the person's character:

- How would your friends describe you?
- How would your work colleagues describe you?

Ask questions about gaps in the CV:

- I notice that there is a gap in your employment history from [date] to [date]. Can you explain the reason?

> **CASE STUDY – Recruit and Select**
>
> Lesley wanted help for her 5-year old daughter Ellie who has Cerebral Palsy and needs 24-hour care with daily living. She asked Jane, her friend, to help as she knows Ellie well. Lesley therefore did not have the expense of recruiting, saved time and was happy she would not have a stranger in her home. Jane agreed verbally that Lesley would tell her at least a week in advance when she wanted her to work.
>
> About a month after their chat, Lesley asked Jane to work on seven occasions as she wanted to concentrate on studying. On four occasions Jane said she could not make it.
>
> Of the shifts she worked, the first shift was after school. Lesley was studying and a half hour before the end of the shift, Jane told Lesley she needed to leave to do some shopping. On the second occasion she left early for an appointment at the hairdresser. The third occasion was a morning shift and she needed to get Ellie ready for school while Lesley prepared for a test. The fourth shift, Jane forgot.
>
> Lesley told her friend that she was disappointed she wasn't committed to the job. Jane was taken aback and said there was no firm agreement and it was not as if she had an employment contract. She told Lesley that it was best she did not continue. They parted and their friendship was strained.
>
> Lesley contacted an agency and after three months she employed an agency worker. She had to pay a fee to the agency. In retrospect, she wished she had asked for professional help with recruiting.

Points to note

Make sure that all parties are clear about the expectations of the work relationship, even if they are family or friends, to avoid unnecessary issues. Recruiting and training a new person is time-consuming, so recruitment must be carried out methodically and fairly. If employed, family and friends should not be given preferential treatment. Using a professional recruiter or HR expert can be a valuable resource. Much work is put into finding the right person, but it is not possible to really know someone until they start working. Not every person selected will be right for the job.

Five Top Tips

1. Carry out the interview with a colleague, such as a case manager or recruiter. People have different views and you may miss something the other person will notice.

2. Follow up an interview with an assessment where you can observe the candidate in the home environment and preferably with the person they will be caring for.

3. Respond quickly to potential candidates. Good people are hard to find and they are not available for long.

4. Consider whether it is appropriate to offer jobs to friends and family. The employment relationship is different from a personal relationship. If you do have family and friends working in the team, agree on some boundaries.

5. Do not discriminate based on age, disability, gender reassignment, marriage and civil partnership, pregnancy and maternity, race, religion or belief, sex and sexual orientation.

2: The Employment Relationship

You have completed your interviewing and you select a candidate you like. What happens next? An offer is made. This may be the beginning of an employment relationship.

An offer can be conditional upon some checks, such as the candidate's right to work in the country, a current Disclosure and Barring Service (DBS) certificate, acceptable references, and a probationary period.

By using an application form as part of the recruitment process, information can be obtained in a consistent format.

An offer, verbal or written, will be binding once it has been accepted, so ensure that you are clear about the terms of the contract of employment before an offer is made.

Adult clients and parents of a child client should be familiar with the contents of the employment contract, or agreement for a worker. They should also be aware of the contents of other procedures and rules of employment, such as a staff handbook and policies or guidance. It is normally the parent who is the first point of contact for employees or workers. This means that they must have some idea of the employer's obligations.

The offer

Make an offer in writing as soon as possible; the following should be included:

- Request evidence of the right to work in the country
- Employer's name and address
- Job title and place of work
- Working pattern – hours/days of work/flexibility
- Pay and benefits
- Ask for information such as bank details for pay, health questionnaire and/or night worker's assessment
- Privacy notice advising how personal details are managed

The contract

All employees and workers have a statutory right to receive a 'statement of written particulars' from day one of employment. For an employee, this will take the form of an employment contract; for a worker, this will take the form of an agreement.

The contract or agreement must, by law, contain minimum details of the employee or worker's terms of engagement as laid down by statute.[4] These are set out in the checklist below.

The type of document issued depends on the relationship that is intended and whether the carer is employed or working on a casual, irregular basis. The employment status can be employee, worker, or self-employed. An 'employee' will have more protection in law than a 'worker', who has more protection or benefits than a self-employed person.

---

[4] A law that has been formally approved and written down (Cambridge Online Dictionary).

The main contracts or agreements are:

1. **Employed on stated minimum hours** means that the employee is guaranteed a minimum number of hours for which they will be paid. The employer has certain statutory obligations to the employee.
2. **Employed on zero hours** means that the employee is not guaranteed any number of hours' work, but the employer has the same statutory obligations to the employee as someone on a minimum hours contract. Holiday will only accrue on the hours worked.
3. **Casual agreements** in the sector are often referred to as 'bank agreements' or zero hours and these are used when a person is needed on an as-and-when basis. These allow flexibility and means that there is no obligation on the part of the employer to offer work, or on the part of the worker to accept work. However, if a pattern is established over time, then it could be said that the relationship is one of employer and employee.

4. **Self-employed people** are not employed; instead, they work under their own company and meet obligations set by the HMRC. A contract for services is agreed between two parties and employment obligations set out in the Employment Rights Act 1996 do not apply. If you intend to work with a self-employed person, speak to an HR expert.

There are many ways of working and the terms of the contract or agreement should be explicit so as not to cause confusion, e.g. part-time, permanent, fixed-term, zero hours, annualised hours, contract for services, apprenticeship agreements, term-time, job share or bank agreement.

Where changes are made to the contractual documents, these must be in writing as soon as possible. These changes are known as variations.

There will be additional rules governing employment that are not set out in contracts but can be noted in other documents, such as a staff handbook or policies. Information will include sickness absence and reporting, disciplinary and grievance rules and procedures, and expectations of 'how things are done around here'. Often these documents do not form part of the contract but there is an expectation that they will be followed.

An employee (not a worker) who requests a contract is protected against dismissal. If an employee is dismissed for asserting a statutory right to receive a statement of their main terms, the dismissal will be seen as automatically unfair. The employee will be able to make a claim at an employment tribunal without having the required two years of employment.

Checklist for the employment contract

- Employer name and address and employee name and address
- The start date of employment and/or the date the employee's continuous employment began
- The method, rate or pay-scale in place for pay calculations
- Pay dates
- Terms and conditions relating to normal hours of work, days of the week the worker is required to work and whether these days/hours vary
- Holiday entitlement and details relating to public holidays
- Holiday pay
- Terms relating to probationary periods (if required), including the length and conditions
- Other paid leave, such as family-friendly leave
- Sick pay and details about incapacity for work
- Employee benefits, such as benefits in kind or financial benefits
- Pensions and pension schemes
- Notice periods for termination of employment by the employer and the employee
- Job title or description of the job
- The expected date a fixed-term contact will end or the duration of non-permanent work
- The address of the normal place of work
- Training provision and requirements
- Collective agreements, if applicable, that affect the terms and conditions of an individual
- Rules relating to disciplinary and grievance procedures

CASE STUDY – Employment Relationship

Maya was a carer for the Taylor family's daughter, Pearl. She was a lovely person but they felt she was not building a rapport with their daughter. Pearl became agitated when Maya worked with her, and Maya did not seem to be able to calm her despite support from other team members.

The Taylors spoke with their case manager, Raymond, who carried out supervision[5] with Maya. Raymond asked Maya if there were any training or support she needed. Maya told him she just wanted to get to know Pearl, which took time, and she did not need any training. Two weeks after the supervision, the Taylors contacted Raymond to tell him that the relationship had not improved. Maya did not fit in, even though the other team members were helpful. She did not take advice from them based on their experience. The Taylors told Emma, the HR adviser, that after six weeks in the job they would expect a carer to reach a certain standard, which Maya had not, even though she had been trained the same as any other new member of the team. They told Emma that they wanted to have her employment terminated.

Raymond discussed the issue with Emma. Emma asked to see Maya's training record and notes of informal meetings or discussions that had taken place. She discussed these with Raymond and the costs and time involved in running a recruitment campaign and training someone new. Raymond felt that they had helped Maya as much as possible through training and support at supervisions, and he agreed with the parents that her employment should be terminated, despite the cost and time involved.

Emma checked the contract for the termination clauses. The probationary period was six months and notice during probation was one week from either the employer or the employee. Maya could be given a week's notice. Emma advised that as a reasonable employer Raymond should hold a probationary review meeting with Maya to explain the circumstances and to bring the employment to an end. After the meeting, Emma asked Raymond to send her the meeting notes and she would prepare a letter to confirm termination.

---

[5] Supervision is a review meeting between a manager and a member of staff.

Points to note

Always check the contract. There are explicit terms, such as the notice period, and 'implied' terms that are not written - such as trust and confidence between employer and employee.
Breaching the terms of the contract may mean that the employee can bring a claim in certain circumstances, especially if they feel the breach was due to a protected characteristic.

The contract must be checked for notice periods and pay in lieu of notice if you don't wish the employee to work their notice. On termination, they should also be paid for any holiday accrued but not taken.

The probationary period is a trial period and where there is no improvement after providing reasonable training and support, then it is reasonable to terminate. The employee also has the opportunity to hand in their resignation at any time if they feel the job is not for them.

Five Top Tips

1. A written employment contract should be given to the employee no later than day one of their employment. The employment contract is examined whenever an issue arises.

2. Contractual terms should be fair, reasonable and in accordance with relevant regulations.

3. Understand the contents of the employment contract, which sets out the basis of the employment relationship.

4. An employee can make a claim to an employment tribunal if the terms of the contract are breached.

5. To encourage a healthy employment relationship, communicate and treat people the way you would like to be treated.

3: The Onboarding Process

In this book, we define 'onboarding' as the work that takes place to bring a new person into the team. In this book it is the time from the point that the candidate is offered a job, and it may include the probationary period. Pre-employment checks are undertaken, induction and training takes place and the new starter is provided with information and guidance on their new job.

After an offer is made to a candidate, it is the recruiter's job to keep in touch with that person on a regular basis. There is usually a gap between offer and start date as the candidate may be working their notice at their current job, or pre-employment checks are being carried out. A friendly 'how are you' during this period helps all parties to start building a rapport.

Onboarding starts with collecting and setting up personal records and collating information, including confirmation of right to work (documents checked at the interview), DBS clearance and references. It is essential to ensure all pre-employment checks are made before the start date.

There are legal requirements, as well as what HR people call 'best practice' to consider. Best practice means going over and above the legal requirements and may help to prevent unwanted financial settlements. It means you will:

- Communicate, obtain feedback, give feedback and provide support so staff understand what you need from them and what they should provide in the service they deliver
- Discuss the contract or agreement with the new starter as early as possible
- Hold regular one-to-one meetings to ensure the new starter has the tools, knowledge and skills to do their job, as well as providing an opportunity for discussions about how things are done in the workplace
- Provide feedback to the new starter on their work and any improvements to be made
- Respond to questions in a timely manner

Personal information is governed by the General Data Protection Regulation 2016. Information must not be kept for longer than necessary; it should not be used for anything other than the purpose it was collected for and must not be shared without consent. See Chapter 8: Keeping Records.

Questions regarding health conditions or attendance should not be asked before an offer is made. An employer may want to ensure that new people are reliable and able to do the work but offers should not be made based on a person's health. If, after an offer is made, information on a health condition, such as a disability, comes to light, an occupational health professional should be consulted before any decisions are made. Can reasonable adjustments be made if the applicant has a disability? If this is not possible, a job offer may need to be withdrawn. This step should not be taken without legal advice.

Checklist for onboarding

- Consider where personal information is held
    - Keep paper documents safe and secure
    - HR software and technology is a good way to retain and manage personal data
    - Employees must keep their personal details up to date, such as address, contact phone numbers and emergency contacts
- Evidence of right to work and DBS checks are carried out according to legal requirements
    - Check that the DBS covers the correct workforce, i.e. child or adult
    - If the new starter is registered on the DBS Update Service, do you have consent to check their DBS?
    - Is the DBS clear without observations?
    - If there are observations on the DBS certificate, who will speak to the new starter about this; this information is sensitive
- Has a pre-employment health questionnaire been requested?

- - Are any adjustments required if the person has a disability?
    - Disclosures must be treated sensitively and considered by relevant professionals
- Have references been obtained from past employers?
    - Are they current/within a reasonable timeframe?
    - Basic information is usually provided; you can ask for relevant additional information, but it may not be forthcoming
- What training is planned over what period?
    - Plan and record when mandatory training is completed and when it should be updated
    - During probation arrange more regular one-to-one meetings
    - If there are issues, discuss them straight away; people will not know what the expectations are if they are not told
    - Where performance, conduct and attitude do not match expectations, provide further training and support
    - Where improvement is not made after reasonable support and training, bring the employment to an end; take advice on how to do this

CASE STUDY – Onboarding

Jacintha applied and was accepted for a job as a support worker with Rashid, an adult with cerebral palsy. Rashid needed support for his daily care as well as his activities. He worked for an IT company and used assistive technology for many of his needs. For example he could tell Alexa to 'vacuum the living room', to switch on the washing machine and lights and to close curtains and blinds. Jacintha had never worked with someone who was as self-sufficient as Rashid.

Rashid preferred to do many tasks himself but Jacintha felt it was her job to do them. Rashid patiently told her that once she sorted the washing and loaded the machine, he would start it when convenient as the noise distracted him. The following week, Jacintha started the machine whilst Rashid was working. He reminded her of their conversation. Jacintha was apologetic. Rashid accepted her apology as she did not work daily and he put it down to her forgetting. A few weeks later, Jacintha worked a Saturday. She started the washing machine when Rashid was still in bed. Rashid was annoyed. He told her she should leave immediately and not continue her shift.

He phoned Emma, his HR adviser. Emma was empathetic and discovered that Rashid hadn't made it clear to Jacintha that when the washing machine was turned on, he wore ear defenders because the noise irritated him. Emma asked Rashid how he felt about Jacintha as a carer. He liked her, they had a good rapport and she had a positive attitude. He was concerned she didn't listen as the washing machine was not the only issue. Emma suggested that she speak with Jacintha, discuss the issues and work with her and Rashid. Emma arranged regular meetings between herself, Rashid and Jacintha to set expectations, and ensure training and knowledge-sharing was carried out and recorded.

Six weeks later, Jacintha had not improved. Rashid was becoming increasingly annoyed; he did not trust that she could carry out his instructions. He asked Emma to bring the relationship to an end before the completion of the probationary period.

After discussing all the details with him, Emma was confident that Rashid's reasons for wanting to terminate Jacintha's employment were genuine and were not due to any protected characteristics such as sex or race. Emma contacted Jacintha to ask her to attend a probationary review meeting the next afternoon.

> At the meeting Emma explained the ongoing issues and that she felt there was little improvement despite the support she and Rashid had provided. Emma asked Jacintha if she had any comments. Jacintha was upset, saying that she was only trying to be helpful. Emma advised Jacintha that the probationary period was a time for both parties to get to know each other and find out if they could work together. She noted that Rashid felt she was a lovely, positive person, but it was important to follow instructions. They had provided her with what they felt was a reasonable timescale in which to improve, but they could not continue, and they had decided to end her employment. Emma confirmed to Jacintha that she would not be required to work her notice but would be paid in lieu, that she would be paid for any accrued but untaken holiday and would receive pay for time worked up to and including the date of their meeting.

Points to note

Onboarding is not only about documentation, but also building the relationship and helping the new starter to embed practices and to understand 'this is how we do it around here'.

The cost of recruitment is not only the recruiter's fee, but the time and effort spent finding the right people. If support and guidance is provided from the start of the employment relationship, but it is clear that the new starter does not fit in and does not meet the standards required, with reasonable training and support, a decision to terminate employment sooner rather than later may be best for all concerned.

Five Top Tips

1. Ensure that employees' personal details, especially in connection with sensitive information related to health, are held securely. These details must not be shared with unauthorised persons without the consent of the employee.

2. Personal records should be in a secure place and must be kept up to date.

3. Undertake pre-employment checks prior to start date.

4. Carry out mandatory staff training and record when it took place and when it should be updated.

5. Go through the main elements of the contract or agreement as early as possible after the start date to set expectations. If expectations are not met it may be best to end the relationship sooner rather than later, but always seek an HR expert's advice.

4: Maintaining the Employment Relationship

Managing people is a skill that is learnt over time. People work best when there is a good relationship with their manager, where trust and respect is shown and given.

Having people who are literally strangers work in your home is daunting. Not many people envisage having help in their home 24 hours a day. It can be overwhelming. Privacy is lost for the individual or family.

It is important to set boundaries with employees at the start of the relationship, to spell out what is acceptable and what is not. Although a home, the house has also become someone's place of work.

Professional staff will know that their code of conduct includes confidentiality and respect for privacy and they will work towards this with your support.

It is natural that relationships form between family and employees, and amongst the staff themselves. As already mentioned, a healthy working relationship is not the same as a friendship. Most working relationships come to an end at some point. How the end is reached can be amicable and develop into a strong friendship, but in some cases the end can be contentious and cause upset. Knowing how to manage employees takes time and effort.

The need for regular communication and trust are implicit in any good relationship and an employment relationship is no different. The employment contract provides the basis for the employer/employee relationship. We have already mentioned in Chapter 2: The Employment Relationship that you must have an understanding of the contents of the employment contract in order to be able to manage expectations.

It is also important that you have someone that you can rely on to provide you with up-to-date employment information and advice; as the saying goes, 'we don't know what we don't know'. The people who can advise and help are the deputy, case manager, HR adviser and other organisations mentioned in Chapter 9: Useful Information.

Training is a huge part of employment. A strong induction is necessary so that employees understand the working environment, the rules of the house, and not least the client's needs. It takes time to settle into a job.

The probationary period allows both parties to learn about each other and discover if they are the 'right fit'. Considerable support is needed in the first few months, and this must be seen as an investment.

How do you keep an open and good employment relationship?

The checklist below provides guidance.

Checklist: maintaining the relationship

- Induction and start of probation
    - Discuss the terms of the contract
    - Advise staff to read the staff handbook, guidance and any policies
    - Plan training
    - Discuss the job tasks, role and responsibilities
    - Arrange regular dates in the diary to review progress
    - Ask for feedback and suggestions
- During probation
    - Discuss conduct or performance issues that do not meet standards as soon as possible and in private
    - Provide further training and support to improve issues
    - Set dates in the diary for regular review meetings to discuss feedback, suggestions, improvements and areas of concern

- Make notes of meetings, review them and, when necessary, ensure that the employee is aware of the concerns or improvements required
- Extend the probationary period if more training or observation is required and if the contract permits
- Bring the employment to an end using the legal procedures if the member of staff does not fit or where they have not met standards despite support
- Confirm the outcome of the probationary review in writing
- Say thank you when it is due
- Acknowledge good work with rewards and incentives
- After probation and beyond
  - Schedule regular one-to-one meetings/reviews/supervisions to discuss client care, employee aspirations and performance and to address any concerns
  - Schedule team meetings to bring people together to share, find work solutions and provide updates
  - Deal with issues in a professional manner by listening, providing constructive feedback and ensuring employees understand the consequences if standards are not met
  - Review current practices, job descriptions, policies and guidance
  - Act reasonably and fairly in all undertakings without discriminating
  - Provide thanks and praise

CASE STUDY – Maintaining the Relationship

Karen, a 10-year-old girl with cerebral palsy, was cared for by a team of three carers. Her mum, Lisa, managed the team, including arranging rotas, pay and holidays and ensuring training. She did a great job but was not always aware of the changes in employment law. She did not have a case manager and instead called upon an HR adviser as and when she needed advice.

Sylvia, a support worker, was contracted to work 40 hours a week and had worked for her for six years. Sylvia did not always take her holiday annually. Lisa had been known to pay in lieu of untaken holiday or to permit Sylvia to take a five-week holiday every second year.

At the end of October Sylvia applied to take the last three weeks of December as holiday and asked Lisa to pay her for the remainder of her holiday. Lisa refused Sylvia's holiday application as it was not convenient for the family and another carer had already booked holiday in the same period. Even though Sylvia provided sufficient notice to take holiday, her contract stated that holiday should be taken when it was convenient for the family.

Lisa suggested Sylvia take her holiday in November. Lisa explained to Sylvia that she could no longer pay her in lieu of holiday as it was not allowed.

Lisa contacted Emma, her HR adviser. Emma said that (a) pay in lieu of accrued but untaken holiday should only be paid to staff who leave employment; and (b) Sylvia was correct that in normal circumstances statutory holiday should not be carried over to the new holiday year. However, she told Lisa that holiday was provided for rest and recuperation and had to be taken during the current holiday year. A portion of holiday could be carried over as Sylvia was unable to take holiday earlier due to staff shortages because of the 2019/2020 pandemic. Sylvia was happy to take her holiday earlier and to carry some of it over. Through communications she understood Lisa's concern for her wellbeing.

Points to note

Everyone needs a break for their own wellbeing. An employer has a duty of care to ensure that staff have sufficient rest and recuperation. This in turn contributes to working safely and people feeling refreshed after a break.

Five Top Tips

1. Provide training and feedback regularly using open communication and tools such as one-to-one meetings and supervisions.

2. If conduct or performance is unsatisfactory, deal with it straight away.

3. Refer to the contract or agreement and staff handbook.

4. When sufficient support and training has been provided and progress is not made despite fair and reasonable support, terminate the employment by following legal procedures and make sure that the reason is not because of a protected characteristic.

5. Seek professional advice.

5: Time off Work

There are numerous reasons why people take time off work. Here, we cover statutory leave; sometimes it is paid and other times it is unpaid. The contract, handbook and policies and procedures should set out how time off is managed and the gov.uk website contains detailed information on this.

Many employment issues stem from the way in which time off is managed. Because every circumstance is different, advice should be sought from an HR expert.

The statutory holiday entitlement for most working people, except for the self-employed, is 5.6 weeks (28 days, which can include the bank holidays) per year. The holiday entitlement is reduced proportionately for part-time staff.

Holiday is paid at a normal rate for staff who work full-time. The calculation of statutory holiday pay for staff who do not work fixed or regular hours is complicated. Their holiday pay will be based on their previous 52 paid weeks to calculate their week's pay.

Managing time off is important as there is a massive impact when staff are absent from work. It has an effect on other members of the team, as well as the family. For instance, if there are three full-time staff who are each entitled to 28 days' annual leave, there will be no staff for 84 days or 12 weeks each year. It pays to manage time off.

The Working Time Regulations 1998 govern working time and breaks. Annual leave is regarded as 'rest and recuperation' on the understanding that, for the sake of health and wellbeing, everyone needs a break.

Annual rest break

Annual holiday is a period of rest and recuperation, and for this reason it is good practice that staff take time off at regular intervals throughout the year and at least one long break of a week.

An employer can require employees to take holiday at times that are convenient to them by giving the employee notice in advance that is double the time they should take off. For example, if the client's family are taking a holiday, they may require only two out of their team of 10 employees to accompany them. The other employees can be given written notice to take holiday at the same time. If the holiday is for seven days, the employees must be given a minimum of 14 days' notice.

Weekly working hours

- The maximum permitted weekly working time is 48 hours averaged over a 17-week period. A worker can choose to work more than the average hours by opting out of the 48-hour week.
- Anyone under the age of 18 should not work more than eight hours in any day, or 40 hours in any week.
- A night worker should not work more than an average of eight hours in 24 hours, normally calculated over a 17-week period.
- Staff who are expected to sleep for most of a sleep-in shift and have suitable sleeping facilities will only be paid the national minimum wage when they are awakened to take care of the client. An employer may provide more favourable pay to attract staff.

Breaks at work

- **Uninterrupted rest break during the day** - minimum 20 minutes if working more than six hours a day. The break is unpaid, unless the contract states that it is paid
- **Daily rest** - minimum of 11 hours rest between working days or shifts
- **Weekly rest** - uninterrupted 24 hours a week or 48 hours in a fortnight

Compensatory rest

Some workers may not be able to take their daily or other breaks if the health and safety of the client is at risk. If the client is on their own and cannot be left alone, it will not be reasonable for a carer to take a break away from the workplace. In these circumstances, the law requires that compensatory rest is provided. For instance, a shift may mean working four long days or nights and having three days off. The bare minimum is 90 hours rest in a week.

Other time off work

There are many situations when people at work will be away. It is not always possible to plan time away, such as sick leave or dependent leave for emergencies. Each situation is different, and the employment contract or staff handbook must be checked for details on what the employer's obligations are to staff regarding time off and whether the leave is paid or unpaid.

There are a number of public duties where there is a statutory reason to grant reasonable time off work where possible. Details can be found on the gov.uk website but these include jury service, trade union duties and activities, and time off for attending training or duty if they are a reservist in the armed forces.

A staff handbook should be provided to staff and accessible in the workplace, either a paper copy or electronically. This normally sets out rules, including information about taking time off to attend medical or dental appointments, what to do when ill, time off for emergencies, what to do if staff are unable to get to work because of bad weather, and who to report absences to.

Family-friendly leave

Parents, including adoptive parents, have statutory rights to leave, some of which have a qualifying period. Partnerships of the same sex also have the right to family-friendly leave. It is important to speak to an HR expert to safely manage leave and pay. Holiday accrues whilst on most family leave and should the member of staff decide that they will not return to work there may be complications if holiday is not documented and managed. Below is a list of family-friendly leave to which staff may be entitled:

- Maternity leave and pay
- Adoption leave and pay
- Paternity leave and pay
- Shared parental leave and pay (SPL)
- Unpaid parental leave - qualifying employees have a right to a total of 18 weeks' unpaid parental leave in blocks of one or more weeks, subject to a limit of four weeks a year
- Time off to care for dependents is unpaid time off and intended to be used for emergencies; no qualifying service is required and this can be taken from day one
- Parental bereavement leave of two weeks is time off for an employee who loses a child under the age of 18, or suffers a still birth from the 24th week of pregnancy

Bad or inclement weather

What are the rules when staff cannot get to work because of the weather? Many employers expect staff to take holiday, whilst others will allow the time to be made up if the time off is not excessive. Ensure that the rules are clear. Always keep records of time off.

Medical appointments

What are the rules for medical appointments? Many appointments are arranged in advance and time off can be requested by the member of staff. This can be taken as holiday or they may swap shifts or work a shift at another time if convenient for all. Wherever possible, request that staff make appointments for when they are not at work.

Contact when away

When staff are unable to get to work, they must know who to contact and by when.

CASE STUDY – Time off Work

Lisa, Karen's mum, noticed that Sandy, who had been working for over two and a half years, began arriving to work every Monday at least 20 to 30 minutes late. The excuses ranged from the weather, to car problems, to oversleeping, or having to take a family member to school, the doctor or the dentist.

Lisa spoke to Emma, the HR adviser. She told her that Sandy was a very good worker, and although 20-30 minutes was not much time off, her continued late arrivals on Mondays made it difficult for her family to organise themselves as they had to cover Sandy's shift.

Emma advised Lisa to arrange a one-to-one meeting with Sandy. She should tell her she had noticed a pattern of lateness, and ask her if there were any problems. Emma told Lisa to then listen and provide Sandy with space to talk.

When asked, Sandy became upset and apologised to Lisa, saying she had not been totally honest about the reasons for being late. She explained that her grandmother had recently moved in with her family. On Monday mornings she helped her grandmother get ready and waited for the transport to take her to the day centre. On other days Sandy's mother was home to take care of her. The transport was often late. Lisa was initially disappointed that Sandy had not explained why she was having unprecedented time off work, but she understood and told Sandy that she must discuss such issues candidly.

Lisa did not want to lose Sandy from the team. The solution was to change her start time. Lisa spoke with the other team members. Together, they came up with a plan that would work for all. The person working the Sunday night shift was happy to start an hour later and end an hour later, which allowed Sandy to arrive on time for her shift. As there was an agreement to the request, Sandy's contract was changed, as was her colleague's.

Points to note

When staff take time off on an unplanned basis, take note of patterns. If the time off is having an adverse effect on the client or the team then deal with it in a non-confrontational way. Listen and ask what help they might need. There may be times when changes cannot be made because it does not suit the family. For instance, if others in the team had similar family commitments and could not be flexible, this situation may have ended differently. Only by communicating can a satisfactory solution be agreed. When a substantial change is requested, use the Right to Request Flexible Working procedure and consult an HR expert.

Health and safety at work

An employer needs to meet certain obligations to ensure that the working environment is a safe place. This includes time off for rest and recuperation. There is a vast range of legislation governing health and safety. The main law is the Health and Safety at Work Act 1974, details of which can be found on the HSE (Health and Safety Executive) website. Health and safety legislation is not covered in this book. However, it is important that employers are aware of their obligations, and regular breaks are important to ensure employees' continued wellbeing.

Five Top Tips

1. Know what the rules are for statutory breaks. If staff are tired or unwell, they will not perform to the standard required, which will affect both them and the person being cared for.

2. Ensure annual leave is taken regularly; an employer can request that staff take leave by giving them notice that is twice the length of the time off that you want them to take.

3. Communicate often - schedule short, dedicated one-to-one meetings to discuss the job requirements and learn what the staff's needs are, such as when they wish to take time off.

4. Tell staff how far in advance time off should be booked so that adequate cover can be arranged. The minimum period is usually stated in the contract. Ensure fairness in approving time off by avoiding informal arrangements.

5. In some circumstances, refusing time off is not legal, such as for emergencies for dependents or attending jury service. If unsure, check with an HR expert.

6: Dealing with Workplace Problems

You make an offer of employment because you like the person and feel they are the right person for your team, they have the right attitude, skills and experience, or they have the potential to be a part of your team. Quite a lot of time and effort is spent on recruitment, and it is costly. When you have problems in the workplace, you'll want to deal with them as quickly as possible so that everyone can move on and concentrate on their job.

It takes different people to make up a team and they need leadership and guidance. Many problems can be avoided by regular communication and setting standards of behaviour and expectations.

When an issue arises, it is best to 'nip it in the bud' quickly. Discuss the issue as soon as possible. Invite the member of staff for a chat or invite them to a supervision meeting. Tell them about your concerns and that their behaviour or performance is unacceptable, and the reasons why. Listen to their point of view.

Tell them what you expect and the consequences of poor behaviour or performance. If you have taken reasonable steps to support staff by communicating and training, and their conduct or performance does not improve, you may need to take formal steps and commence the disciplinary procedure. The outcome of such a procedure can be a verbal warning, first or final written warning, or a dismissal.

The law protects employees from unfair dismissal, from discrimination, bullying and harassment, as well as violations of health and safety.

If an employee has a concern about the workplace, another member of staff or the employer, they may raise a grievance. The procedures set out in the staff handbook or the ACAS Code of Practice must be followed. This means investigating, listening at a meeting, and offering an appeal if they are not satisfied with the outcome.

A disciplinary procedure can be invoked to deal with an on-going conduct or performance issue.

Different people should carry out different parts of the disciplinary. Ideally, one person would carry out the investigation, another would chair and hear the allegation at a disciplinary and the complaint at a grievance, and a third would be appointed to hear an appeal if required. For instance, the case manager might carry out the investigation. If an HR expert carried out the investigation, the case manager might hear the disciplinary or an HR expert could be appointed. The appeal could be heard by an independent HR expert, or you could contact the Citizens Advice Bureau or ACAS for advice.

Do not discuss matters of a disciplinary or grievance with anyone who does not need to know or be involved. Maintain confidentiality and privacy.

Talk to an HR expert for advice on drafting documents and chairing meetings and hearings, and for guidance through the procedure.

The ACAS Code of Practice sets out the disciplinary procedure. Where there are conduct or performance issues, try informal talks, training and, if necessary, a verbal warning. Take a look at Chapter 4: Maintaining the Employment Relationship. Where there is no improvement, steps should be taken, such as commencing the formal disciplinary procedure.

Checklist for dealing with a grievance

- Check the grievance procedure and follow it
- Discuss complaints and try to resolve them; keep notes
- If the matter is recurring, enquire whether the staff member wants to bring a grievance
- Invite them to a meeting, inform them of the right to be accompanied and the opportunity to appeal
- Listen carefully at the meeting, ask relevant questions
- Take notes at the meeting or agree that it will be recorded
- Provide the employee with a copy of the notes or recording if the meeting is recorded
- Make a decision as soon as possible after the meeting and advise the employee in writing of the outcome
- Ensure that they understand the outcome and that the matter has ended; if they are not in agreement, suggest they raise an appeal

Checklist for dealing with a disciplinary

- Check the disciplinary procedure and follow it
- The person appointed to investigate should speak with the employee concerned to check facts, speak to witnesses and carry out reviews of relevant documents
- An HR expert should be consulted to decide if there is a case to answer
- Invite the employee to a meeting; this should be in writing
- The letter should include date and time, venue, the allegations, invitation to be accompanied by a colleague or trade union representative, and the opportunity to appeal

- The employee should be provided with all relevant documentation to support the allegations; they must have an opportunity to prepare their response
- State what the potential sanctions might be, for example written warning or dismissal
- Provide at least 48 hours' notice; be prepared to postpone should the employee request time to arrange to be accompanied
- Ensure that the person who hears the disciplinary is not the same person who carried out the investigation
- Agree if the meeting is to be recorded or if notes will be taken, and provide the employee with a copy
- Do not make decisions before the disciplinary hearing
- Advise the employee of the decision in writing as soon as possible after the hearing
- Ensure that they understand the possible consequences of repeat misconduct or underperformance
- An appeal should be heard by an independent party and not the investigator or the person hearing the appeal; let the employee know who they should address their appeal to
- Mistakes in procedure may result in financial loss due to claims being brought for unfair dismissal, or if the employee believes they were discriminated against
- Seek advice from an HR expert

Checklist for dealing with an appeal

- Check the grievance or disciplinary procedure, whichever is applicable
- An appeal must be received in writing
- An independent party should be appointed to hear the appeal - someone who has not previously been involved in the disciplinary or grievance
- The appeal must be arranged in a timely manner
- A written invitation must be sent for someone to attend a meeting
- The letter must include date and time, venue, the name of the person who will hear the appeal, and a note that they may be accompanied
- Provide at least 48 hours' notice and be prepared to postpone should the employee request a delay to arrange for a colleague to accompany them
- Hold the meeting, ensuring that the employee has any new information if further investigations have been carried out
- Advise the employee of the outcome as soon as possible
- The decision is final

CASE STUDY – Workplace Problems

Bobby, a 7-year-old, acquired a brain injury soon after birth. His parents had responsibility for his care, under the auspices of a deputy. They employed five permanent special needs carers and had two workers for ad hoc cover. Bobby lived with his mum, Georgina, his dad, Johan, and two siblings. Theirs was a very busy household.

Georgina did not have time to go out and meet other people. She tended to confide in the carers, mainly Mary, the team leader. Mary had worked with Bobby for two and a half years and understood the fine line between being an employee and a friend. Georgina shared some views about her relationship with her husband in confidence with Mary, who felt uncomfortable. Mary decided to talk to Johan about it. When Georgina went to fetch the other children from school, Mary took the opportunity to suggest to Johan that he speak with Georgina. He was offended as he felt she was interfering in their private life and told her to get out of his house. Mary left, not knowing what else to do. She felt she had done the right thing by bringing the matter up with Johan.

That evening Georgina phoned Emma, their HR adviser, as they did not have a case manager. Emma contacted Mary and, after listening to her, placed her on paid leave whilst she further considered the matter. Georgina was adamant that she could not have Mary back in the home as she said Mary had breached her trust and confidence.

After careful consideration, Emma decided to dismiss Mary on the grounds of some other substantial reason (SOSR) as the parents had lost trust and confidence in Mary and it was impossible for the working relationship to continue.

Points to note

In the next chapter, we see how the dismissal of a member of staff for conduct or capability or on the grounds of redundancy are potentially fair reasons to dismiss. However, there are other situations where it can be fair to dismiss employees. This is where there is 'some other substantial reason' for a dismissal. For example, if an employee refuses to accept terms of employment, in the case of personality clashes or conflict of interest, or pressure from a third party. Dismissal for SOSR is also discussed in the following chapter.

Five Top Tips

1. Before taking steps to terminate employment, consider all the facts. Is the desire to terminate a knee-jerk reaction or the result of careful consideration?

2. Check the disciplinary procedure and follow it, even if it appears to be time-consuming. This is much better than facing a claim at an employment tribunal.

3. Check that the reason for termination is not discriminatory and has nothing to do with the employee having one or more of the protected characteristics.

4. Ensure that the employee has been provided with the opportunity to explain their position. Listen to the employee and consider if any decision made is fair and reasonable.

5. Seek expert advice early to prevent unnecessary stress and financial loss.

7: Leaving

Everything has an end, including an employment relationship. In legal terms this is referred to as a 'termination', but there are many different ways for an employment relationship to end.

There can be serious implications if you get this wrong. An employee can bring several claims if they feel they have been dismissed unfairly. However, an employee with less than two years' service cannot bring an unfair dismissal claim.

Wherever possible, the employee should be aware that their employment may be terminated. Actions to support, provide training or warnings should, as far as possible, be provided before dismissal takes place.

There are five potentially fair reasons to dismiss an employee: capability, conduct, redundancy, breach of statutory restriction and some other substantial reason.

An employee may terminate their employment by giving notice to resign or retire. Below, we discuss the following:

- Resignation
- Retirement
- Dismissal (fair and unfair)
- Redundancy
- Some other substantial reason (SOSR)

Managing a leaver is as important as managing someone starting work. Obtain advice from an HR expert whenever you consider exits from employment, especially where you have not carried out a procedure, such as investigating, holding a meeting and offering an appeal, and where the employee has been working for more than two years.

Resignation

When an employee tells you they want to leave, this is a resignation, and they should provide you with notice as set out in their employment contract. An employee should not feel they have been provoked to resign. They should not feel they had no option but to tender their resignation. If this is the case, they may bring a claim to an employment tribunal that could result not only in financial loss, but impact the morale of the team, the family and the multi-disciplinary team (MDT) (the professionals advising or providing care, such as a physiotherapist, speech therapist, occupational health, social services). A resignation provides an opportunity to take stock of the workforce. Who is needed? Are any changes required? If so, consider these before recruiting.

Checklist for dealing with resignation

- Request the resignation in writing
- Check the date of leaving, accrued and untaken holiday and how or when other team members will be informed
- Agree whether notice will be worked or they will be paid in lieu and leave early
- Accept the resignation in writing, confirming the notice period and date of leaving, holiday pay or requirement to take holiday during the notice period
- What handover is needed – does any property or documents need to be returned?
- Remind the employee of confidentiality and privacy clauses in the contract
- Arrange final pay
- Where it might be helpful, an exit interview or meeting can help to understand why people are leaving and what improvements might be made
- Confirm the best way to contact them, such as email address, telephone number or physical address, should anything need to be sent on
- If a reference is required it must be factually correct

Retirement

Since the default retirement age was removed in 2011, employers can no longer retire employees. The employee can choose to retire when they are ready. However, there may be reasons why retirement is necessary and, if this is the case, the employer must be clear about the reasons so that they can defend them should a discrimination claim be brought on the grounds of age. If performance levels drop, it might be a fair reason to encourage retirement based on capability. However, before any steps are taken an HR expert must be consulted.

Checklist for dealing with retirement

- Notice should be in writing
- Check the date of leaving, accrued and untaken holiday and how or when other team members will be informed
- Agree whether notice will be worked or they will be paid in lieu and leave early
- Accept the resignation in writing, confirming the notice period and date of leaving, holiday pay or requirement to take holiday during the notice period
- What handover is needed – does any property or documents need to be returned?
- Remind the employee of confidentiality and privacy clauses in the contract
- Arrange final pay
- Celebrate the retirement and thank the employee for their contribution

Dismissal

When an employer wishes the employee to leave, they will 'dismiss' following specific procedures. A dismissal can be fair or unfair.

A fair dismissal includes:

- An investigation, the outcome of which could be a disciplinary hearing
- A meeting to hear the employee's response to the allegations
- Invite the employee to bring someone with them to accompany them in the meeting
- Allow an appeal if they don't agree with the decision

Follow the ACAS Code of Practice on disciplinary and grievance procedures.

If the employer does not follow the process, they could find they are facing a claim for unfair dismissal. This can involve an excessive amount of time and financial loss.

If a fair dismissal has not been carried out, for whatever reason, seek advice from an HR expert. See Chapter 9: Useful Information for organisations that can help.

Checklist for dealing with dismissal

- What is the reason for the dismissal, is it fair?
- What reasonable support and training has been provided?
- Has the employee been warned that employment may come to an end?

- Who will be involved in the dismissal, for instance, who will investigate, who will chair the disciplinary hearing and who will hear the appeal?
- How will the message that the employee has left be communicated to colleagues?

Redundancy

A potential redundancy can occur when a job role is no longer needed, or there is not enough work for the employee in a particular job due to a change in circumstances, or the location of the job changes significantly. For example, a job may be at risk of redundancy if a move to a different home means employees need to travel further than is reasonable. Another example is if the care package requirements change, for instance, waking night shifts are needed and day shifts are no longer necessary. The job of waking night shifts will then be at risk of redundancy.

It is important to follow the step-by-step process in managing redundancies, no matter how many staff are affected. Obtain advice from an HR expert as early as possible to involve staff in a consultation process. Be sure that there is a justifiable reason for the redundancy and the reason is not associated with the protected characteristics mentioned above.[6]

Communication is crucial during a redundancy process, and it is important to listen to suggestions from employees to consider whether redundancies can be avoided. Advise employees of decisions in a timely manner throughout the consultation

---

[6] The protected characteristics are: age, disability, gender reassignment, marriage and civil partnership, pregnancy and maternity, race, religion or belief, sex and sexual orientation.

process, such as who is selected for redundancy, the termination payments and date of termination, or discuss alternative employment.

When an employee has worked for more than two years, they may be eligible for a statutory redundancy payment. Seek advice from an HR expert or payroll provider for calculating termination payments when an employee is made redundant.

Mistakes in the redundancy procedure could result in financial loss to the client. There may be a basic award that is calculated in the same way as a redundancy payment, in addition to a compensatory award.

What happens when sadly a client dies?

When someone we know passes, it is a sad time for the people left behind. Each of us deals with loss differently. We are not normally prepared for death even though we know it is a part of living.

If the person who is being cared for in your home dies, what happens to the care staff? This book is about employment, and it would be remiss of me if this important stage were ignored.

On the death of the person being cared for, the job role for the care staff disappears. In employment law terms, there has been a *frustration of contract*. This means that the contract cannot continue by either party because the terms of the contract cannot be fulfilled. As the job is no longer available it is a redundancy situation. This is a fair reason for dismissal.

It is important to contact the HR expert as soon as possible to discuss the steps to be taken.

Some care staff may have been working for many years in the job and they will experience an acute sense of loss, not only because they no longer have a job. They may grieve for the person who they have come to know and love and will miss the relationship with the family. Communicate and stay connected with the staff through this period or ask someone else to contact them if you are unable to do so.

Funds are often frozen when someone dies. This means that it could take weeks or months before staff receive their contractual pay and any termination benefits such as statutory redundancy pay.

Each case will be different and if a deputy is appointed, they may be the best person to ask.

Checklist for dealing with redundancy

- Is there a clear, justifiable reason for the redundancy?
- What costs are involved?
- Who are the people who will be affected?
- Plan the process using a timeline, such as:
    - Date for announcement
    - Plans for individual consultation meetings
    - Date the redundancy will become effective
    - Scripts needed for meetings
    - Letters needed for the employee
    - Calculations for end of employment payments
    - How and when to communicate to others
- What criteria will be used to select for redundancy?
- What alternative roles, if any, can be offered to avoid redundancy?

Some other substantial reason (SOSR)

A dismissal under SOSR must be 'substantial' and not insignificant. Each case will be different and the circumstances of the reason for dismissal should be considered carefully.

It is important to make sure that 'some other substantial reason', whatever it is, is the main reason for the dismissal. Could the reason be one of the other fair reasons for dismissal, such as conduct or capability (performance or sickness)? If so, dismissal on the grounds of SOSR will not be relevant or fair.

Once the reason is clear, consideration needs to be taken of what is reasonable given the circumstances of the case, the employment environment, the size of the team and other factors pertinent to the employment.

Some examples of SOSR dismissals are where there is pressure from a third party, if the employee refuses to accept new terms of employment, personality clashes between employees or between employee and employer/parents that cannot be resolved, conflict of interest or expiry of a fixed-term contract. It is important to obtain advice from an HR expert before taking steps to dismiss under some other substantial reason.

Checklist for dealing with SOSR

- Has every reasonable effort been made to find an alternative to dismissal, including communicating with the employee?
- Has due process been followed?
- Obtain advice from an HR expert

Dismissal of a worker

The position is entirely different when someone who is on the list of casual workers is no longer required. If you intend to bring the arrangement to an end, either stop offering work or terminate the agreement. Either way, there are no legal restraints, as long as the employer does not discriminate.

However, care must be taken to make sure that the relationship is still that of worker and an employment relationship has not inadvertently been created, thereby giving the worker the same legal rights as an employee. See the section 'Permanent Employee or Worker' in Chapter 1: Recruit and Select.

CASE STUDY – Leaving

Miriam was employed as a buddy to Shirley, who lived with her mother, Evie. Shirley had been involved in a car accident and acquired brain injury. Before her injury, she was a bright chemistry graduate in a multi-million dollar corporate and doing very well on the graduate programme. She enjoyed physical activity such as cycling, swimming, climbing as well as socialising with family and friends.

She lost the confidence and ability to carry out many of these activities after the accident. With Miriam's help, she had begun to regain confidence. Miriam enjoyed her part-time job working three weekends a month. She loved the outdoors and was delighted to assist in Shirley's rehabilitation programme, which included taking her swimming, cycling and climbing.

Miriam decided to apply to and was accepted at a university some miles from Shirley's home. Because she worked weekends she continued as her shifts fitted in with her university timetable.

At the start of her second year at university, Miriam asked the family if she could work Fridays instead of Sundays for three months. This did not suit the family but they agreed to rearrange their plans so they could accommodate her request. Evie changed her plans temporarily to visit her aged mother who lived a two-hour drive from her. It was preferable to visit on Sundays and not Fridays due to her mother's routine at the residential home and traffic conditions.

When Miriam came to work on the last Friday of the three-month temporary arrangement, she asked if the change could be permanent. Evie told Miriam that it was not convenient, and she expected her at work on Saturday and Sunday from the following weekend.

Miriam came to work on Saturday but at the end of her shift she told Evie she could not work on Sundays. Evie told her that she didn't have a job if she couldn't work on Sundays. Miriam sent a text to Evie on Sunday morning letting her know she wouldn't be there. Evie text back saying she didn't have a job and she should not come back to their home. She would pay her whatever was owed to her.

Miriam contacted her Citizens Advice Bureau (CAB) who advised she had been unfairly dismissed, having worked for five years a procedure was not followed and she wasn't given notice. Shirley's parents consulted their HR expert and, after prolonged discussions between the parties, a settlement was reached by mutual agreement.

Points to note

Had Evie consulted her HR expert before dismissing Miriam, she would have been advised to work through a procedure and Miriam might then have been dismissed fairly. Miriam could have used the Right to Request Flexible Working procedure to ensure the change was considered fairly and she had an opportunity to make suggestions. In the circumstances, Evie's action had an impact on the family as they felt pressured, moral was low, and they had to pay settlement compensation, although not astronomical. This might have been avoided if Evie had discussed the situation with her HR expert.

Five Top Tips

1. Follow procedure.

2. Treat people the way you would like to be treated.

3. Listen - there may be another way.

4. Take expert advice early to prevent unnecessary stress and financial loss.

5. Have an independent person carry out exit interviews, if the circumstances permit, especially when staff resign, to analyse reasons for leaving and if improvements can be made.

8: Keeping Records

All that paperwork! But it really doesn't have to be a lot of paperwork if you understand what records need to be kept and why.

Technology abounds and where you can make use of it safely, it's a good idea to do so. Many people use devices and apps where they manage data on the Cloud. In this way, HR software solutions and timekeeping applications are easily accessed from anywhere to make managing processes easier. When employees have access to systems they can keep their personal details up to date, employers will have records that are correct, and this frees up administration time. Using software as a service also frees up valuable space that would otherwise be taken up with filing cabinets or drawers.

The General Data Protection Regulation 2016 governs the collection, use and retention of people's personal data. It's important to remember that data is provided for specific purposes and should be used for those purposes only.

It is best not to share personal information such as phone numbers and addresses with others, unless specific consent has been provided. HR is normally the keeper of personal data. Some of this data will be shared with payroll or other persons on a need-to-know basis.

Data such as number of days of sickness, absence or health disclosures are classified as sensitive. When an employee discloses such information, for instance in a health questionnaire, that information should not be shared unless the employee has provided explicit consent.

An employee does not need to volunteer the fact that they have a medical condition, but they must answer questionnaires honestly. Disclosing medical conditions may be in the employee's best interests if reasonable adjustments need to be made. Personal information such as the fact that someone is pregnant should also not be shared except with the pregnant employee's permission.

Keep personal details in a safe place for as long as the information is needed. Most employment information should be kept for six years after the employee leaves; some information may be kept longer depending on the circumstances. Check with an HR expert as different legislation applies to different types of records. When providers are changed and personal data is exchanged, for instance between different HR providers or different case managers, the employee should be made aware of who is receiving their data.

It is important to keep records that show that statutory or best practice has been followed in case a claim is brought at some future date, especially where there has been conflict or termination.

When applicants apply for jobs, there is quite a bit of information gathered at the interview. This should be kept for at least six months as an unsuccessful job applicant may bring a claim if they feel they were discriminated against during the process.

The Information Commissioner's Office (ICO) regulates the management of personal data. Any company that controls data in the UK should be registered to this organisation.

CASE STUDY – Keeping Records

Emma, the HR adviser, was asked by a deputy's office to provide HR support for Rashid, a 35-year-old man who had multiple complex disabilities. Rashid's deputy set up a trust, and his sister, Salma, was one of the trustees. Salma managed Rashid's care and his staff. He had a team of six permanent carers and three workers.

Emma sent a quarterly newsletter to her clients. One of the newsletters set out how variable-hours workers should be paid for their holiday breaks and what rates of pay should be applied. Having read this, Salma was led to believe that she may have been underpaying staff for their holiday. Salma discussed the matter with Emma, who was asked to assist with a solution.

Salma went through her records with Emma. It took some time for Emma to understand the paper records. She provided Salma with information about an IT-based HR system, advising that it would help to ensure the records kept were correct and stored safely. The administration time for managing timesheets and rotas would decrease substantially. Emma explained that the software, if used correctly, would allow a report to be sent to payroll with all the correct information required to calculate holiday pay, as well as the normal pay requirements.

Salma understood that this would help reduce the risk of people being overpaid or underpaid, reduce the time required to administer the payroll, and help to keep her records up-to-date and correct; most importantly, it would free up her time to concentrate on managing the care of her brother.

Five Top Tips

1. Only collect personal data for specific reasons and advise the employee of the reason.

3. Use technology to manage data, keep it up to date and secure, permit employees to amend their personal details and access personal documents, handbooks, policies, and guidance documents, and ensure consistency in administration.

4. Only keep data for as long as it is necessary.

5. Destroy personal data securely.

9: Useful Information

Employing people should be satisfying for both employer and employee. There is much information on this that can help. Further detailed information is available from many organisations and we have listed a number of them below. Space has been left so local information can be added.

> ACAS or Citizens Advice Bureau for impartial employment advice
>
> HMRC for information on employment status and statutory payments
>
> Gov.uk – the government website with information on all things related to employment
>
> HSE – for all things health and safety
>
> Information Commissioner's Office (ICO)
>
> DBS (Disclosure and Barring Service)
>
> Right to Work Check – Share Code
>
> Skills for Care – Code of Conduct
>
> Your local social services *[add your own details]*:
>
> Your local environmental officer *[add your own details]*:
>
> Your own useful information *[add your own details]*:

Has the book been informative?
Did you like what you read?
Leave a review
Sign up to receive our newsletter for useful tips
and notifications of further books in this series
go to
www.hilfranpublishing.com

Follow our Facebook Page: Hilfran Publishing
Follow us on Twitter: HilfranPub

10: About the Author

Cecily Lalloo is an HR professional with over 25 years' experience advising and supporting small to medium sized businesses (SMEs). She studied Employment Law, Employee Relations, Management Development and Resourcing at Buckinghamshire New University in England and is a Chartered Member of the CIPD.

She worked as HR Manager for 12 years in an SME, then decided to start a consultancy to help SMEs who do not need a full-time HR professional. Early in her company's development she was introduced to the world of case management associated with complex care for clients in their own homes. She works with deputies, case management companies and independent case managers.

Cecily has built a reputation for providing HR advice and support to this niche market and, with her team of HR experts, she also works directly with parents and adults who do not have case managers.

Her objective is to educate families on an employer's obligations when people work in their homes. She is aware of the sensitivities that this brings and the trauma that people in this situation have already been through. She understands that many would prefer not to have people working in their homes 24 hours a day, but realises that the carers, personal assistants and buddies are helping them and their loved one who needs the care.

Cecily's aim is that the *Employing Positively Series* of books and audio books will assist in best practice employment that helps to retain and develop staff for the long-term. In today's world, care is a valuable commodity and the people who deliver care need to be nurtured, developed and cared for themselves.

Having worked with many families whose children have acquired brain injury, Cecily's wish is to set up a sensory room for children with brain injuries in her home country of Zimbabwe. For each publication that is sold, £1 will be donated to fulfilling this dream.